THE WONDER
OF READING
**Literacy Grant
2010 - Isleton Library**

AMERICAN HUMANE

Protecting Children & Animals Since 1877

Beginning Pet Care

WITH AMERICAN HUMANE

Learning to Care for a

HoRSE

Felicia Lowenstein Niven

Bailey Books
an imprint of
Enslow Publishers, Inc.
40 Industrial Road
Box 398
Berkeley Heights, NJ 07922
USA
http://www.enslow.com

AMERICAN HUMANE

Protecting Children & Animals Since 1877

Founded in 1877, the American Humane Association is the only national organization dedicated to protecting both children and animals. Through a network of child and animal protection agencies and individuals, American Humane develops policies, legislation, curricula, and training programs — and takes action — to protect children and animals from abuse, neglect, and exploitation. To learn how you can support American Humane's vision of a nation where no child or animal will ever be a victim of abuse or neglect, visit www.americanhumane.org, phone (303) 792-9900, or write to the American Humane Association at 63 Inverness Drive East, Englewood, Colorado, 80112-5117.

To our Readers:

We have done our best to make sure all Internet Addresses in this book were active and appropriate when we went to press. However, the author and the publisher have no control over and assume no liability for the material available on those Internet sites or on other Web sites they may link to. Any comments or suggestions can be sent by e-mail to comments@enslow.com or to the address on the back cover.

Every effort has been made to locate all copyright holders of material used in this book. If any errors or omissions have occurred, corrections will be made in future editions of this book.

Bailey Books, an imprint of Enslow Publishers, Inc.

Copyright © 2011 by Enslow Publishers, Inc.

Library of Congress Cataloging-in-Publication Data

Niven, Felicia Lowenstein.
 Learning to care for a horse / Felicia Lowenstein Niven.
  p. cm. — (Beginning pet care with American Humane)
 Includes bibliographical references and index.
 Summary: "Readers will learn how to choose a horse and care for a horse, from what kind of horse is best for them and how long they live"—Provided by publisher.
 ISBN 978-0-7660-3196-8
 1. Horses—Juvenile literature. I. Title.
 SF302.N58 2010
 636.1—dc22

                              2008048961

Printed in China

052010 Leo Paper Group, Heshan City, Guangdong, China

10 9 8 7 6 5 4 3 2 1

Illustration Credits: All animals in logo bar and boxes, Shutterstock. Associated Press, p. 36; Blair Seitz/Photolibrary, p. 27; © Carol Walker/naturepl.com, p. 16; David R. Frazier/Photo Researchers, Inc., p. 43; Gerald & Buff Corsi/Visuals Unlimited, Inc., p. 28; Jodie Hanson, p. 7; Juniors Bildarchv/Photolibrary, p. 22; © 2009 Jupiterimages Corporation, pp. 3 (thumbnail 2), 11; © Mark J. Barrett, p. 41; Megan McDonough, pp. 3 (thumbnail 1), 4-5; Michelle Del Guercio/Photo Researchers, Inc., p. 38; Shutterstock, pp. 1, 3 (thumbnails 3, 4, 5, 6), 14-15, 17, 18-19, 20, 23, 25, 26, 30, 33, 34-35, 39, 42; © Tom Carter/PhotoEdit, p. 29.

Cover Illustration: Shutterstock (close-up of brown and white horse).

Table of Contents

Emily rides Rocky at
4-H camp.

Chapter 1

Rescue

The first thing that the girls noticed was the limp. It was the kind that would not go away, they were told. That is why the horse's owner was ready to give him up.

The horse, Rocky, was well named. The brown and white "paint" had lived a rocky life. He had been passed from one home to another and still another. At only five years old, Rocky had a limp from being overworked. He needed surgery to fix it.

Rescue

The girls looked at their 4-H leader, Susan Sheridan. She had just started Bay State Equine Rescue, Inc. Would Rocky be their first rescue horse?

Sheridan nodded. But she knew that it would take a lot of money to pay for the surgery.

The girls talked it over. Their town had a can and bottle recycling program. Maybe they could collect enough cans and bottles for the operation.

It took four months to raise the twelve hundred dollars needed. But they did it! Rocky had his surgery. His leg was put into a cast to heal.

One of the other 4-H members knew exactly what that felt like. Ten-year-old Emily had recently broken her arm. She had fallen off of a horse. Her mom decided that Emily needed to learn more about horses, including how to ride safely. She enrolled her daughter in 4-H.

Rowan and her horse Echo.

Rescue

Emily formed a special bond with Rocky. She groomed him and took care of him. She took riding lessons with him. When Rocky was healthy again, Emily's family adopted him.

Today, Rocky is a happy, healthy horse. He is a featured part of the tour at the family's maple syrup business, Hardwick Sugar Shack.

"Horses like Rocky used to pull sleds in the old days," said Megan McDonough, Emily's mom. "But Rocky doesn't have to work anymore. He can just enjoy life."

Emily works hard, however. She gets up at five o'clock each morning to give Rocky his hay, grain, and water. She also cleans his stall and grooms him. Each day, in return, when Emily gets off the school bus, Rocky whinnies "hello."

Emily is not the only person who has given a good home to a horse. Twelve-year-old Rowan Hanson had always loved horses. That is why

Rescue

someone made a donation in her name to a horse rescue. The group, New England Equine Rescues (NEER), sent Rowan a card to let her know.

Rowan checked out the group's Web site. What she saw made her cry. She was determined to help. So she put posters and collection cans around her school. In about two months, Rowan raised more than one thousand dollars!

Rowan's donation was used to save a big black Tennessee Walking Horse. His grandfather had been a champion.

fast facts

Emily gets up at five o'clock each morning to give Rocky his hay, grain, and water. She also cleans his stall and grooms him. Each day, in return, when Emily gets off the school bus, Rocky whinnies "hello."

Rescue

"He was so skinny," remembered Rowan. "But I loved him the instant I saw him. We went to the paddock and he followed me around."

The rescue group brought the horse to foster care. It was just a mile from Rowan's house. She was able to visit him and help care for him.

It was not long before Rowan and her family adopted him. She named him Echo, because it seemed to fit him.

Today, Rowan and Echo are best friends. "He'll do anything for Rowan," said mom Jodie. "She's even training him to barrel race."

"Echo is so lucky," said Rowan. "He went through such a hard time and now he's in a safe place. But I think I'm really the lucky one—because I have him."

Kids like Emily and Rowan can make a real difference in the life of a horse.

Chapter 2
History of the Horse

It is hard to imagine what life was like more than 50 million years ago. But that is when scientists think the first horses walked around. These animals did not look like horses at all. They were more like foxes or dogs. Their feet even had pads like a dog's but the pads ended in hooves.

An ancient cave drawing found in Spain showing a horse.

History of the Horse

Scientists are not sure what happened next. From the fossils they found, it seemed that these small creatures became more horse-like over time. Some had many toes. Some had few. Some grew large. Others stayed small.

fast facts

The first horses were more like foxes or dogs. Their feet even had pads like a dog's but the pads ended in hooves.

One kind, however, started to look like the horses we know today. This happened about a million years ago. We think that these pony-sized animals galloped around North America. They had single hooves on their feet and long, flowing tails. They traveled with a herd. They acted like wild horses.

Then, less than ten thousand years ago, these early horses became extinct in North America.

History of the Horse

Luckily, some of them were also in Asia. Those horses grew to become the ones we know today.

Humans discovered quickly that horses were very useful. Horses could carry people over long distances. They could pull heavy loads. They could help people hunt more effectively. They could help them fight in wars. They also could live happily with people. Horses became a prized possession.

When the Spanish explorers came to America, they brought their horses. Once horses returned to North America, they quickly became comfortable here. They grew into herds of horses.

Today, tens of thousands of wild horses live in North America. Still others are owned by loving families. And many are working horses. But all share something in common. The horse will always have a special place in our history, and our hearts.

13

Chapter 3
Getting a Horse

Clydesdale

In the United States, horses have different roles. Some work on farms, pulling equipment. Others work in cities, pulling carriages. Still others help to herd sheep or cattle. But most horses are not used for work. They belong to people who like to ride them, show them, or race them. If you are thinking about getting a horse, you most likely want one for these reasons.

Are you ready for a horse? There is a lot to know before you make this decision.

It can be expensive to keep a horse. If you do not have your own land, you will need to find a place for your horse.

Palomino Morgan

That can cost hundreds of dollars each month. Then there is the money for food. Horse owners can spend more than one hundred fifty dollars each month on hay, grain, and other food. There is also medical care. It can cost about six hundred dollars a year for a healthy horse, and much more if your horse gets sick.

You must have time to care for a horse. That means traveling to the stable and feeding your horse at least twice a day. You will need to clean out

Getting a Horse

the stall. You will need to groom your horse. You will need to exercise him.

Are you strong? Do you have a lot of energy? You will need both. You will be carrying buckets of water and armfuls of hay. You will be raking stalls. You will be lifting saddles. You have to do this work every day, including holidays. It is your responsibility if you have a horse.

You may think you are ready. Now how can you find the right horse?

Horse feed

There are more than two hundred fifty breeds of horses and ponies in the United States. They range from the big Clydesdales to the smaller Morgan and Arabian horses. Different breeds are good at different things.

17

Getting a Horse

A large draft horse is strong but not fast. But you might choose him to pull a carriage. If you needed to herd sheep, you might select a quarter horse. That breed is known for its speed for short distances. A book on horse breeds can tell you which ones might be a good fit.

Another way you can choose a horse is by its size. While humans measure height in feet and inches, horses are measured in hands. One hand is equal to four inches. A horse is measured from the ground up to the highest point on his withers. This is the place between his shoulders. Horses are usually at least fourteen-and-a-half hands, which is fifty-eight inches. Anything smaller is considered a pony.

Getting a Horse

Are you a good rider or just beginning? Make sure that the horse matches your riding skill. If you are not sure how to train a horse, you should get one that is already trained.

Also, look at the horse's temperament, or personality. Is he calm and steady or easily excited? If you are just beginning, look for a horse that is easy to handle.

Finally, you have to think about the horse's age.

If you plan to ride your horse, make sure you wear the proper safety equipment such as boots and a helmet.

Getting a Horse

Older horses are usually calmer. But they could have bad habits. They also could have medical problems. Ask questions to learn as much as you can.

Where can you find a horse? Your local 4-H Club can tell you. You can also ask local horse trainers. You can find them at horse shows. You can look up horse rescue groups on the Internet. There are a lot of homeless horses that need a good home.

Be prepared to spend a lot of time choosing your horse. Meet each horse, ride it, and take the time to see if it is a good fit.

It is a good idea to have your new horse checked out by a veterinarian. You can find one in your local yellow pages. Not all small animal vets will care for large animals like horses. You might need to call a few vets to find out. You may also want to ask your stable for recommendations.

Make an appointment with your vet as soon as

Getting a Horse

you can. The nice thing is that you do not have to bring your horse into a vet's office. The vet will come to you.

On the first visit, the vet will examine your horse. He will listen to her heart and lungs. He will check her teeth and hooves. He will watch your horse walk and trot. He may do a blood test. If vaccines are needed, he will give those shots.

The vet visit is also the time for you to ask questions. Write them down so you do not forget what you want to know.

When you first get your horse, it is very important to have a vet examine her.

Chapter 4

Health and Exercise

Imagine that you are the proud owner of a new horse. Are you ready to bring him home?

You need a stall in a stable, or a pasture and safe shelter, to keep your horse. You will need to clean that stall every day.

You will need a clean stable. This is where you horse will stay.

Health and Exercise

That means getting rid of the manure, or poop, to prevent conditions that could cause health problems for your horse.

Many horse owners use a pitchfork to remove the wet and dirty hay. They shovel it into a wheelbarrow. Then they wheel it over to the manure pile. If you use sawdust or shavings, you might want to buy a shovel instead. You might also want a broom to sweep it clean. Those are just some of the cleaning supplies.

You also need to keep your horse well fed. A horse will eat about twenty pounds of food a day. He will drink about twelve gallons of water per day, on average. But your horse will not do that all at once. Horses like to graze, or eat a little at a time. You need to make sure that your horse has hay or grass to nibble on throughout the day. He also needs to have fresh drinking water available. You can give him some grain, too. Check with your vet

Your horse will need to eat small amounts of food throughout the day.

for the proper amount of each type of food to give your horse.

You want your horse to be clean and comfortable. That means there should be grooming supplies on your list. Many horse owners use several different kinds of brushes. One is a currycomb to loosen dirt.

25

Another is a body brush with stiff bristles. A third is a comb for the tail and mane.

Do not forget about the hooves. They collect a lot of dirt. You will want a hoof pick to clean out the inside. Also, horse hooves grow and need to be trimmed, just like our fingernails. Make sure to schedule a visit from a farrier. He can trim the hooves. He can also put horseshoes on to help protect them.

Your horse will also need fresh drinking water every day.

The list is already long, but it is not finished yet. You will need supplies in order to ride your horse,

To keep your horse clean, be sure to groom her.

or even lead him around. A halter is a harness that slips over a horse's head. It can be attached to a rope so you can lead him.

A bridle is like a halter, but it is used to guide your horse while you are riding. It has reins that you can hold. It also may have a piece of metal or rubber, called a bit, that fits in the horse's mouth. When you pull on the reins, the horse feels it in his mouth.

A farrier will trim the horse's hooves and place horseshoes on them.

Your horse will need daily exercise. Riding a horse is good exercise for you, too!

Before you ride your horse, you need proper equipment.
It is also a good idea to take riding lessons.

Health and Exercise

Or you can use a hackamore halter, which guides the horse without a bit. If the horse is trained, he will know what to do when you pull on the reins of either type.

Of course, you do not ride bareback. That is why you need a saddle with stirrups and a saddle pad.

Most importantly, do not forget your safety gear. Safety is very, very important. As a rider, you need to wear boots. They will protect your feet. They also have a heel that will help you hold down the stirrups. Then you need a riding helmet. This protects your head if you should fall.

Those are the basic supplies. They will help keep you and your horse safe and healthy.

So will regular visits from the vet. Horses usually see the vet once a year. Those older than twenty should see the vet twice a year.

Your vet is also your horse's dentist. Did you know that a horse's teeth never stop growing?

Health and Exercise

As horses eat, their teeth wear down. Your vet will make sure your horse's teeth are not too long, too sharp, or too short. He will help prevent any chewing problems.

A healthy horse will need daily exercise. You can ride for fun, of course. But you might want to take lessons. That way, you can train your horse at the same time. You might even want to compete with your horse. There are horse shows for beginners as well as more advanced riders.

One great place to find out more about horses is your local 4-H chapter. There you will meet other kids who love horses.

Chapter 5
Problems and Challenges

O wning a horse is fun. It is also challenging. You may face some problems. Some of these will be health problems. Others may be behavior problems. Knowing about them will help. Here are some examples of common ones.

Horses graze on grass. They can sometimes get sick. Check your horse every day for signs of illness.

Health Problems

Remember that horses graze on grass. That is an easy way to pick up parasites. These are tiny living things that could upset their stomachs. They may include roundworms, tapeworms, and pinworms. If your horse has problems going to the bathroom, that could be a sign of a parasite. You may not know whether your horse has a parasite. But your vet can test the horse's poop.

Fly and tick bites are another type of problem. You might notice sores on your horse's legs, neck, or head. Your vet can give you lotions or sprays. Keeping your horse clean will also help.

Always watch your horse for signs of illness. Horses cannot tell you they are sick

Your horse should have plenty
of room to roam in a pasture.

Problems and Challenges

but you can usually notice. Do you smell anything bad around his hooves? This could be a sign that there is a problem. Is your horse walking in a funny way? He may have hurt one of his legs. Is he tossing his head a lot? He could have an infected tooth. If your horse is behaving differently, it could mean he is not feeling well.

Check and brush your horse's teeth. A vet or groomer can also do this for you.

Behavior Problems

You might also notice some bad behavior. Understanding the causes can help you to stop it.

Your horse may show some behaviors that you may think to be aggressive. Examples include biting, kicking, and charging at other animals or people. If you notice these behaviors, contact a professional.

Bucking is another behavior problem. This is when the horse kicks its hind legs up in the air. If the horse has a rider, this is dangerous. Bucking could be caused by playfulness. In that case, the horse has to be trained. Also, check your saddle. Sometimes the horse bucks to tell you that the equipment is not a good fit.

Wood chewing is another behavior problem. Some horses chew the wood in their stalls.

Problems and Challenges

They may be bored, or they may be missing something in their diet. If your horse chews wood, talk to your vet about this problem. Also, try to exercise him more often.

These are just some challenges that you may find. Even though they are not medical problems, you can ask your vet for advice. If she cannot help, she can refer you to someone who can.

Taking good care of your horse may help behavior problems. Ask your vet for help if you are unsure of what to do.

Chapter 6

A Lifelong Responsibility

Horseback riding can be fun for the whole family!

Horses often live into their twenties and thirties. That means when you buy a horse, he will be around for a long time. If you are willing to care for him, he will give you so much in return.

A Lifelong Responsibility

Horses keep us active and get us out of the house. Caring for a horse is good exercise. So is riding one. Plus, you get to spend time in the great outdoors. All of these are benefits of owning a horse.

Horses can improve our mood. It is hard to be lonely or sad when your horse happily greets you. They may even help us make new friends who also love horses. In this way, they reduce stress. They help to make us happier people.

Horses are good for us in other ways. They teach us responsibility. They help us to feel good about ourselves. After all, we are able to take care of a horse. That is quite an accomplishment!

Plenty of people take care of horses because they love these animals. Famous people now and throughout history have formed close relationships with them.

William Shatner, who played the original Captain Kirk on *Star Trek*, loves horses! He founded the

A Lifelong Responsibility

Hollywood Charity Horse Show that takes place each spring in Los Angeles. His favorite breed is the American Saddlebred.

Joe Montana, who used to play quarterback for the San Francisco 49ers, also rides and shows his horses. He likes to compete in cutting horse shows. That is where he practices the cowboy skill of "cutting" a herd of cattle into small groups.

Actress and singer Hilary Duff, and her sister Haylie, have a special attachment to horses.

Horses make people happy.

A Lifelong Responsibility

They grew up with them on their Texas ranch. Hilary started riding when she was just four years old. She and her sister had Shetland ponies named Cinnamon and Sugar.

A horse can be an important part of your life, too. You do not have to be famous. Simply spend the time to ride him and care for him. Make a difference in his life and you will have a friend forever.

Shetland ponies make good pets, too!

Horses live a long time. Make sure you have the time,
money, and energy to care for a horse. If you do, your
horse will be an important part of your life.

Glossary

bit—A piece of metal or rubber that slips into a horse's mouth; pressure from the bit tells the horse which way to turn and when to stop.

bridle—A harness that slips over a horse's head and is used by the rider to control the horse.

farrier—A person trained in hoof care and shoeing.

graze—To eat a little bit at a time; in the case of horses, usually grass or hay.

halter—A harness that slips over a horse's head to lead him or her around.

hand—The measurement unit for a horse, equal to four inches.

hoof/hooves—The hard part of a horse's feet.

mane—The flowing hair along the neck of a horse.

parasite—A tiny living thing that feeds off another living thing.

reins—Straps attached to the bridle that the rider uses to guide the horse.

rescue group—A group of people that finds homes for homeless animals.

saddle—A leather seat especially made for people to ride on horses.

stable—A building for farm animals with separate stalls.

stall—A compartment in a building for farm animals.

stirrups—Places to put your feet when riding; stirrups hang down from the saddle on either side of the horse.

vaccine—A shot to prevent disease.

veterinarian ("vet")—A doctor specializing in animals.

withers—The highest part of a horse's back, between its shoulder blades.

Further Reading

Books

Clutton-Brock, Juliet. *Horse*. New York: DK Children, 2008.

Decaire, Camela, and Michelle Watkins. *Girls and Their Horses*. Middleton, Wisc.: American Girl Publishing, Inc., 2006.

Funston, Sylvia. *The Kids' Horse Book*. Toronto, Ontario, Canada: Maple Tree Press, 2004.

Gaff, Jackie. *I Wonder Why Horses Wear Shoes: And Other Questions About Horses*. Boston: Kingfisher, 2006.

Kimball, Cheryl. *Horse Showing for Kids: Training, Grooming, Trailering, Apparel, Tack, Competing, Sportsmanship*. North Adams, Mass.: Storey Publishing, 2004.

Langrish, Bob. *The Horse Breeds Poster Book*. North Adams, Mass.: Storey Publishing, 2003.

Further Reading

Internet Addresses

4-H

    <http://www.4-h.org>

American Humane Association

    <http://www.americanhumane.org>

# Index